# John Thompson's Modern Course for the Piano — FOURTH GRADE

# CHRISTMAS PIANO SOLOS

ISBN 978-1-4234-5692-6

WILLIS MUSIC

EXCLUSIVELY DISTRIBUTED BY

HAL•LEONARD®

Visit Hal Leonard Online at
**www.halleonard.com**

Contact Us:
**Hal Leonard**
7777 West Bluemound Road
Milwaukee, WI 53213
Email: info@halleonard.com

In Europe contact:
**Hal Leonard Europe Limited**
Distribution Centre, Newmarket Road
Bury St Edmunds, Suffolk, IP33 3YB
Email: info@halleonardeurope.com

In Australia contact:
**Hal Leonard Australia Pty. Ltd.**
4 Lentara Court
Cheltenham, Victoria, 3192 Australia
Email: info@halleonard.com.au

# Contents

# Mistletoe and Holly

*Use with John Thompson's Modern Course for the Piano*
*FOURTH GRADE BOOK, after page 6.*

Words and Music by Frank Sinatra,
Dok Stanford and Henry W. Sanicola
*Arranged by Eric Baumgartner*

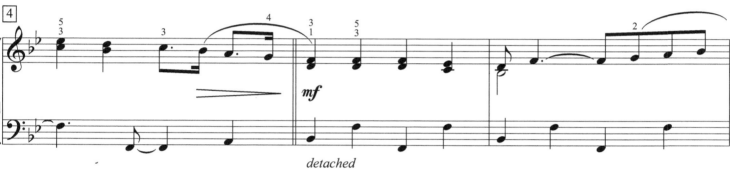

# Blue Christmas

*Use after page 15.*

Words and Music by Billy Hayes
and Jay Johnson
*Arranged by Eric Baumgartner*

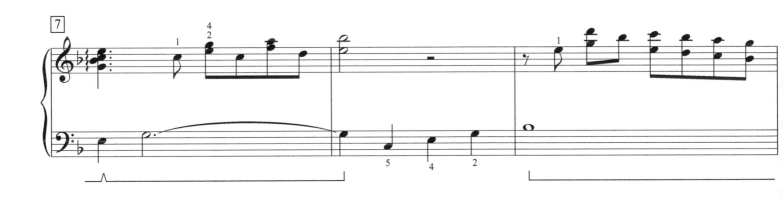

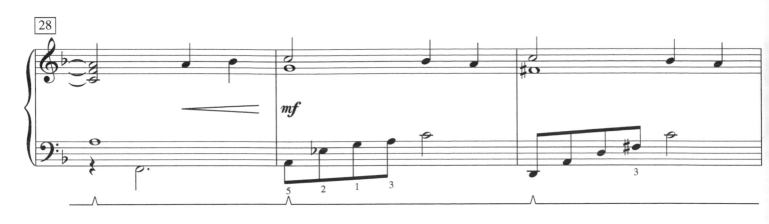

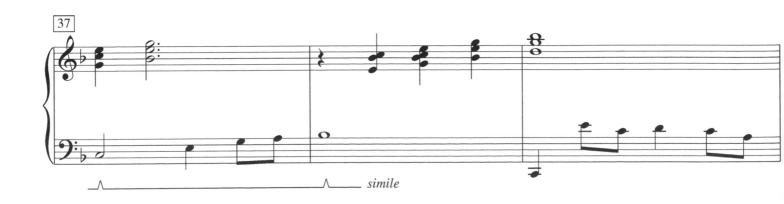

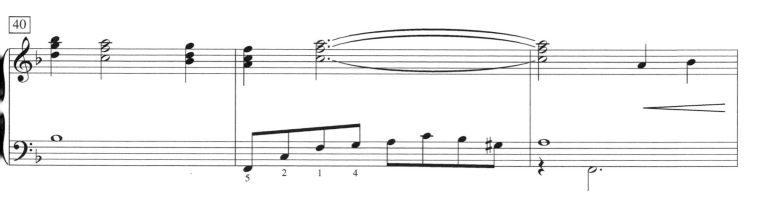

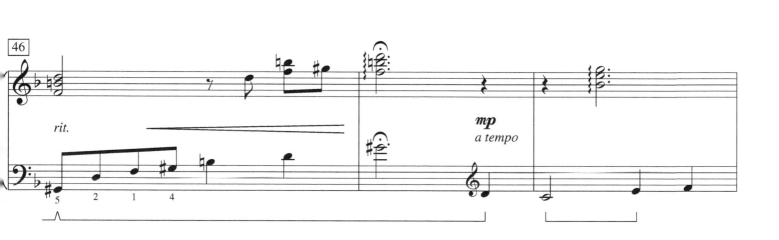

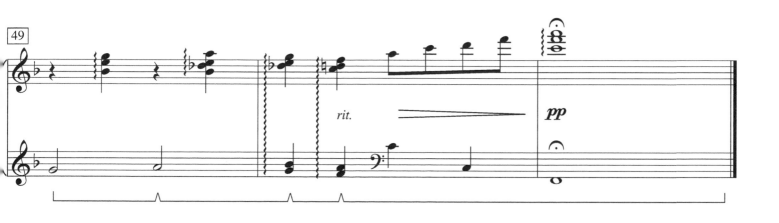

# The Most Wonderful Time of the Year

*Use after page 19.*

Words and Music by Eddie Pola
and George Wyle
*Arranged by Eric Baumgartner*

Bright Waltz tempo

# Rockin' Around the Christmas Tree

*Use after page 33.*

Music and Lyrics by Johnny Marks
*Arranged by Eric Baumgartner*

# I Wonder as I Wander

*Use after page 39.*

By John Jacob Niles
*Arranged by Eric Baumgartner*

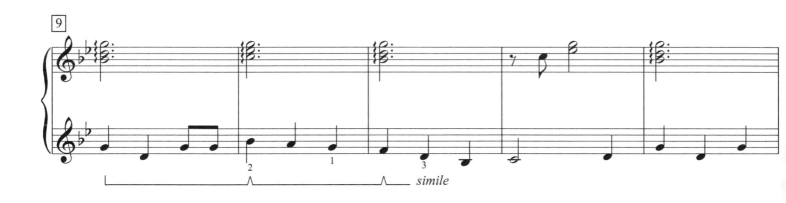

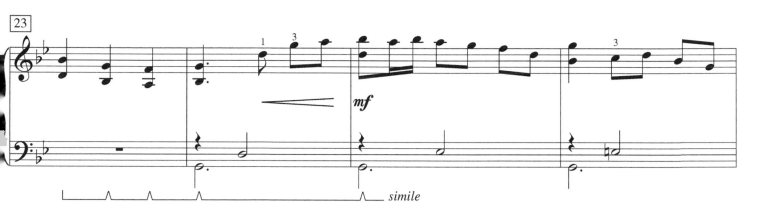

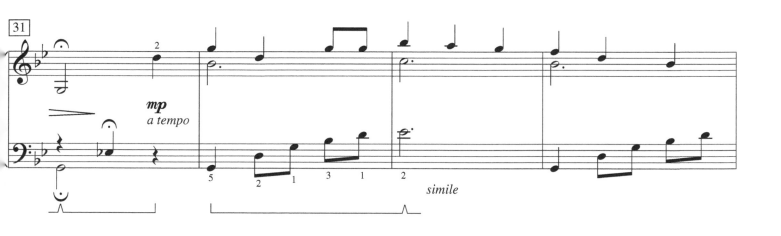

# Feliz Navidad

*Use after page 43.*

Music and Lyrics by José Feliciano
*Arranged by Eric Baumgartner*

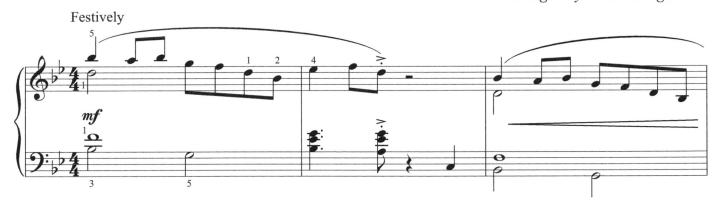

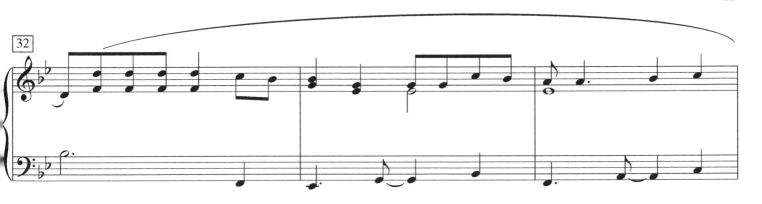

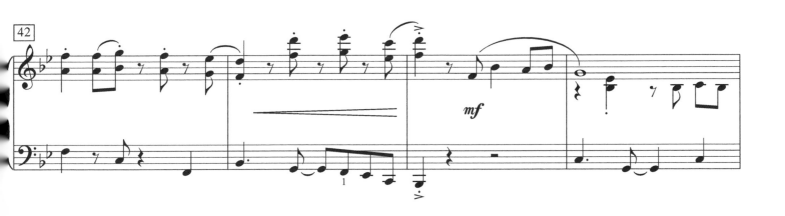

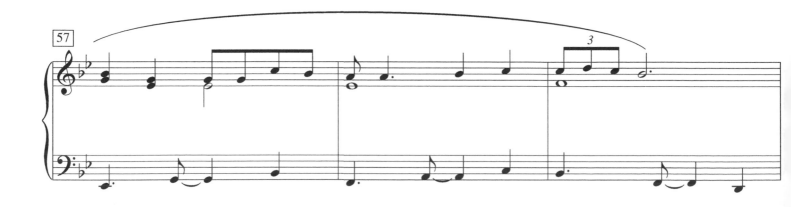

# Santa Claus Is Comin' to Town

*Use after page 57.*

Words by Haven Gillespie
Music by J. Fred Coots
*Arranged by Eric Baumgartner*

# Silver Bells
## from the Paramount Picture THE LEMON DROP KID

*Use after page 71.*

Words and Music by Jay Livingston
and Ray Evans
*Arranged by Eric Baumgartner*

*sempre legato (with occasional pedal)*

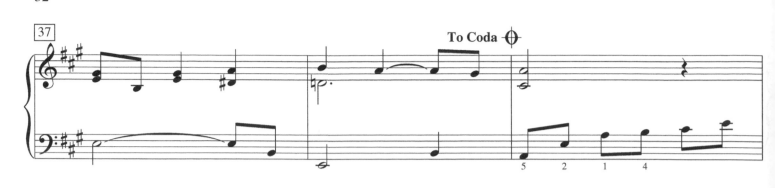

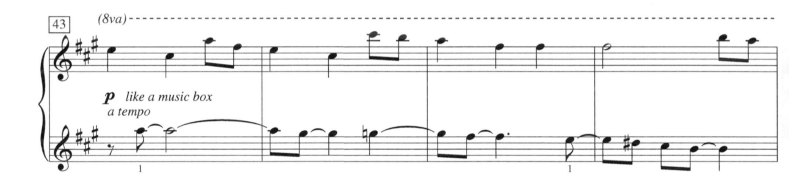

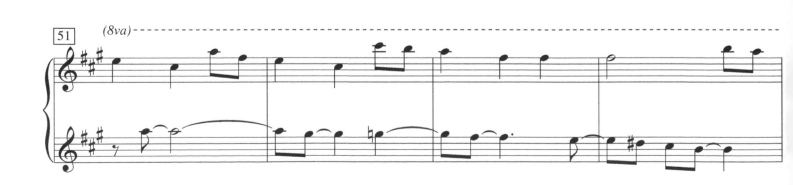

# The Christmas Song
## (Chestnuts Roasting on an Open Fire)

*Use after page 83.*

Music and Lyric by Mel Tormé
and Robert Wells
*Arranged by Eric Baumgartner*

Expressively, with much warmth

*With pedal (sempre legato)*

# Some Children See Him

*Use after page 92.*

Lyric by Wihla Hutson
Music by Alfred Burt
*Arranged by Eric Baumgartner*

Eric Baumgartner's *Jazz It Up! Series* are jazz arrangements of well-known tunes that both experienced and beginning jazz pianists will enjoy. The stylized pieces are intentionally written without chord symbols or improvisation sections, although pianists are encouraged to experiment and explore!

  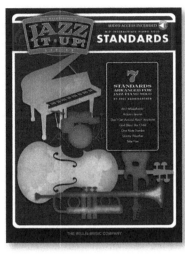 

## Christmas
### Six Carols
*Mid-Intermediate Level*
Deck the Hall • God Rest Ye Merry, Gentlemen • O Christmas Tree • The Coventry Carol • Good King Wenceslas • Jingle Bells.
**00416752 Book/Audio ... $9.99**

## Familiar Favorites
### Seven Folk Songs
*Mid-Intermediate Level*
All Through the Night • The Erie Canal • Greensleeves • La Cucaracha • Londonderry Air • Scarborough Fair • When the Saints Go Marching In.
**00416778 Book/Audio ... $9.95**

## Classics
### Six Classical Faves
*Mid-Intermediate Level*
Funeral March of a Marionette (Gounod) • Habanera (Bizet) • Nutcracker Rock (Tchaikovsky) • Song for the New World (Dvořák) • Spinning Song (Ellmenreich) • Symphonic Swing (Mozart).
**00416867 Book/Audio ... $9.99**

## Standards
### Seven Favorite Classics
*Mid-Intermediate Level*
Ain't Misbehavin' • Autumn Leaves • Don't Get Around Much Anymore • God Bless' the Child • One Note Samba • Stormy Weather • Take Five.
**00416903 Book/Audio . $12.99**

View sample pages and hear audio excerpts online at www.halleonard.com

WILLIS MUSIC

Prices, contents, and availability subject to change without notice.

0817

# CLASSICAL PIANO SOLOS

## Original Keyboard Pieces from Baroque to the 20th Century

Compiled and edited by Philip Low, Sonya Schumann, and Charmaine Siagian

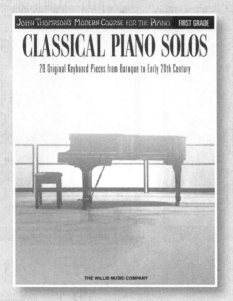

### First Grade

**22 pieces:** *Bartók*: A Conversation • *Mélanie Bonis*: Miaou! Ronron! • *Burgmüller*: Arabesque • *Handel*: Passepied • *d'Indy*: Two-Finger Partita • *Köhler*: Andantino • *Müller*: Lyric Etude • *Ryba*: Little Invention • *Schytte*: Choral Etude; Springtime • *Türk*: I Feel So Sick and Faint, and more!
00119738 / $6.99

### Second Grade

**22 pieces:** *Bartók*: The Dancing Pig Farmer • *Beethoven*: Ecossaise • *Bonis*: Madrigal • *Burgmüller*: Progress • *Gurlitt*: Etude in C • *Haydn*: Dance in G • *d'Indy*: Three-Finger Partita • *Kirnberger*: Lullaby in F • *Mozart*: Minuet in C • *Petzold*: Minuet in G • *Purcell*: Air in D Minor • *Rebikov*: Limping Witch Lurking • *Schumann*: Little Piece • *Schytte*: A Broken Heart, and more!
00119739 / $6.99

### Third Grade

**20 pieces:** *CPE Bach*: Presto in C Minor • *Bach/Siloti*: Prelude in G • *Burgmüller*: Ballade • *Cécile Chaminade*: Pièce Romantique • *Dandrieu*: The Fifers • *Gurlitt*: Scherzo in D Minor • *Hook*: Rondo in F • *Krieger*: Fantasia in C • *Kullak*: Once Upon a Time • *MacDowell*: Alla Tarantella • *Mozart*: Rondino in D • *Rebikov*: Playing Soldiers • *Scarlatti*: Sonata in G • *Schubert*: Waltz in F Minor, and more!
00119740 / $7.99

### Fourth Grade

**18 pieces:** *CPE Bach*: Scherzo in G • *Teresa Carreño*: Berceuse • *Chopin*: Prelude in E Minor • *Gade*: Little Girls' Dance • *Granados*: Valse Poetic No. 6 • *Grieg*: Arietta • *Handel*: Prelude in G • *Heller*: Sailor's Song • *Kuhlau*: Sonatina in C • *Kullak*: Ghost in the Fireplace • *Moszkowski*: Tarentelle • *Mozart*: Allegro in G Minor • *Rebikov*: Music Lesson • *Satie*: Gymnopedie No. 1 • *Scarlatti*: Sonata in G • *Telemann*: Fantasie in C, and more!
00119741 / $7.99

### Fifth Grade

**19 pieces:** *Bach*: Prelude in C-sharp Major • *Beethoven:* Moonlight sonata • *Chopin*: Waltz in A-flat • *Cimarosa*: Sonata in E-flat • *Coleridge-Taylor*: They Will Not Lend Me a Child • *Debussy*: Doctor Gradus • *Grieg*: Troldtog • *Griffes*: Lake at Evening • *Lyadov*: Prelude in B Minor • *Mozart*: Fantasie in D Minor • *Rachmaninoff*: Prelude in C-sharp Minor • *Rameau*: Les niais de Sologne • *Schumann:* Farewell • *Scriabin*: Prelude in D, and more!
00119742 / $8.99

---

The *Classical Piano Solos* series offers carefully-leveled, original piano works from Baroque to the early 20th century, featuring the simplest classics in Grade 1 to concert-hall repertoire in Grade 5. An assortment of pieces are featured, including familiar masterpieces by Bach, Beethoven, Mozart, Grieg, Schumann, and Bartók, as well as several lesser-known works by composers such as Melanie Bonis, Anatoly Lyadov, Enrique Granados, Vincent d'Indy, Theodor Kullak, and Samuel Coleridge-Taylor.

- Grades 1-4 are presented in a suggested order of study. Grade 5 is laid out chronologically.

- Features clean, easy-to-read engravings with clear but minimal editorial markings.

- View complete repertoire lists of each book along with sample music pages at **www.willispianomusic.com**.

The series was compiled to loosely correlate with the *John Thompson Modern Course*, but can be used with any method or teaching situation.